the fire
of love

the *fire*
of love

A MEMOIR

ELI JAXON-BEAR

NEW MORNING BOOKS, ASHLAND, OREGON

The Fire of Love: A Memoir
by Eli Jaxon-Bear

© 2025 Eli Jaxon-Bear

First Printing 2025

New Morning Books, Ashland, OR U.S.A.
(541) 201-0900
www.newmorningbooks.com

Edited by: Julie Maurer and Leigh Estok
Cover and Interior Design: Chris Molé, Book Savvy Studio
Cover photo: Michael Waha

Library of Congress Control Number: 2025905002
ISBN: 979-8-9928833-0-5

Printed in the United States of America

Dedicated to my life partner and lover,
who has dedicated her life to us.
A gift from the Goddess and a goddess in form.
I owe everything to her grace,
ferocious clarity and loyalty.

***

Contents

Fire of Love:
From Cancer's Ward

PROLOGUE: SEPTEMBER 12, 2001

I flew from San Francisco into New York as the towers burned. Our flight was the lone aircraft permitted to land that day. Perhaps the airspace was opened for the President to fly in and our flight slipped in as well? Our footsteps echoed through an empty JFK Terminal where only armed military personnel stood watch. That evening, I conducted my scheduled radio show on WBAI, powered by emergency generators.

I had flown into a war zone. To see the towers burning as we flew in at dusk was a memory forever burned into my mind. I saw that the people in Manhattan had been blown open as well, revealing basic goodness. Strangers shared and helped strangers, hotels took in people with nowhere to go. For the first time in my life, being born in Brooklyn and growing up in Queens, I felt New York as a full community—all of us in this together.

I cherish these precious moments. I first felt the elation of true community during the civil rights demonstrations on the streets in Montgomery, Alabama. The same wartime-like pressure, with mounted klansmen charging into us, and the Deacons for Defense, armed with shotguns, guarding the church where we slept on the floor. Barriers melted and joined us together heart to heart, as we sang freedom songs.

On the twentieth floor of my two-week rental, I opened the doors to a small balcony facing downtown with a view of the burning carnage. Just then, a gust of wind blew in the most toxic smell I have ever encountered.

I never thought anything could smell as toxic as the steel mills. They burned sulfur, coal, lime, and coke in the quarter-mile of open ovens. The heat needed to melt steel into liquid radiated heat waves of smoke that combined with the exhaust from steam engines, jack hammers, and fork lifts, to belch out a filthy dark cloud every day, every hour, non-stop. That was our daily environment while working in Open-Hearth 4, one of Andrew Carnegie's original steel mills in Pittsburgh.

But the smoke that blew into my open patio door wasn't ground level smoke filled with dirt and dust that may cause disease, lung cancer, or death from inhalation. This smoke came from a fire still burning high up on the tower, mixing molten jet fuel, wires, melted and vaporized plane, building, and humans. This toxic brew turned out to be a gene-altering shock to the human form.

My partner, Gangaji, flew in a week later for our weekend at Riverside Church on the Upper West Side. With everyone shaken and shattered and blown open, we sat together in silence and love and overflowing bliss. We all recognized each other as having the potential for being the light of love in the midst of fear and darkness.

A few days into the chaos, while first responders were still fighting the fires, President Bush went on TV and literally asked that we all "go back to shopping." He then announced that America would embark on a "crusade." People went back to shopping and America went on an imperial crusade called "The War on Terror."

In a blink of an eye, the United States was running secret torture prisons, violating international law and everything that we had stood for as a nation; the final blow to our integrity, self-esteem, and self-image as a people.

The ascendance of Trump is a sign that the terrorist wound in the country's psyche on 9/11 had metastasized. A sociopathic madman was now a societal cancer two decades later.

My cancer also needed time to metastasize and start melting my bones.

The seeds planted that September day would take years to fully bloom—both in the nation's psyche and in my own body. But, for me, the first crack had appeared two years earlier, in a seemingly innocent encounter that would change everything.

THE FIRE
OF LOVE

The Seeds of Despair

Two years before 9/11, Bush had been instrumental in my life. Before the burning towers, before he was president, he unknowingly helped to trigger my personal downfall, presaging the country's moral collapse that was to come.

In the fall of 1999, I flew to Portland, Oregon, for a book tour. I ended up in the same hotel as George W Bush, who was there for a campaign rally and Republican fundraiser. When I looked out my hotel window there were SWAT teams with weapons on the rooftops looking into my room. The halls were filled with cigar smoke and the raucous sounds of drinking and partying. I felt I had stumbled onto a rung of hell, not knowing it was a taste of what was to come. I couldn't wait to get out onto the street, explore the city, and breathe the smoke-free air.

It was a warm September evening and the bookstore was crowded to overflowing. As I was just beginning, a baby held in the lap of a young woman cried and interrupted my opening. I restarted and the baby cried again. The woman, without saying a word, left with her child, and I felt immediate gratitude for her kindness in letting the meeting proceed.

I was happy with the meeting and the response of the people present. I was there to share my teacher's transmission of the possibility of freedom, of direct self-realization through a quiet mind and an open heart. There were many people open and ready to receive the good news that night. I signed a stack of books and slipped out on my way to the Thai restaurant next door.

Standing under a tree on the sidewalk was the same woman with her daughter. I didn't notice her at first as I passed by, but she called out to stop me.

"Where are you staying?" she wanted to know. I told her the name of the hotel. "Oh, that's terrible," she said. "Let me make you a home-cooked meal. You can hang out at my place and tell me what I missed in there."

She caught my eye and for a moment I lost my guard, surprised by the light shining in her eyes. With her baby on her hip and her scarves, beads, and long dress, she looked like a street kid refugee from my old commune, and I felt something move inside of me. I couldn't believe myself. Some part of me wanted to take her up on her offer. I dreaded returning to the hotel, was at a low point in my relationship with my partner, and she somehow evoked old images and desires from an earlier part of my life. How easy it would be to say "yes," and follow her home. No one would know. What harm could there be?

But I knew better. Since meeting my teacher in 1990, I had been blissfully celibate for nine years and I was not interested in a return to the suffering of a life run by my sexual passion. I had had enough sex in those early commune days to last a lifetime. Now I was married, in a committed relationship, and even though we were going through hard times, I deeply loved my partner and was not interested in anyone else.

I thanked her for her offer and let her know that if she really wanted to hear what I had to say, that she could have a scholarship to my weekend starting the next day. That first movement, which seemed so innocent at the time—an offer of help to someone in need—was the first movement of sentimentality, subconsciously flavored by desire. She wrote down her phone number and address and pressed it into my hand.

I left for the restaurant, never expecting to see her again. As I ate, I looked at the paper and wondered at her spelling of "my haus." Was she possibly German, a bad speller, or just eccentric? I left the paper behind when I left the restaurant and headed back to the hotel.

She showed up at the weekend, sat in the back unnoticed and never said a word. In the final round of questions and answers, she raised her hand and I recognized her from the evening before.

"Would you move in with me?" she asked from the back of the room. I had never been asked anything remotely like that before. Where did she come from? I smiled and said, "As love, I am already alive in your heart. Check and see."

With that, I left town and never gave her a second thought. But the seed had already been planted. I was already in trance.

> *Nothing is real.*
> *All else comes and goes.*
> *Nothing is certain.*
> *All else a gamble.*
>
> *Meet emptiness with Silence*
> *And all is revealed.*

My next stop was Boulder, and she somehow came to that weekend. I didn't notice her, and she only told me about it a year later when I returned to Portland. She was now on the volunteer team that brought me back and she was my driver. For the next three years, she organized and led the Portland volunteers, showing up wherever I was teaching. I saw her serving selflessly and I was becoming attached.

It was the days of cassette tapes, before CDs, and she sent me a mix tape that blew my mind. The music was pitch-perfect and exactly my taste. From John Coltrane's *Too Young to Go Steady*, to early Dylan and every genre I loved from bluegrass to blues, Rasta to Woody Guthrie and more. She had captured over an hour of music from my past. It was a psychic seduction and it got to me. It ended with *Eli's Coming*.

How could she know me so deeply? How could she know the music of my time when she was still just a baby? I sent her a message telling her that she was my "music goddess" and asked how she collected this tape. She replied that she copied them off of the radio and said she preferred "music mistress."

When Gangaji returned from leading a retreat, I tried playing the tape for her. She brushed it off with a warning to be careful. But it was too late. I had already crossed the line. I had fallen in love. I had thought I was over such feelings. Years of celibacy had shown me the bliss of peace and quiet and the follies of the sexual arena. After all, Gangaji and I had weathered nearly three decades together, building a life neither of us could have imagined when we first met in Bolinas that summer of 1976. To understand the magnitude of what was at stake—what I was about to lose—you need to know where this story really began.

Love's Journey

Long before the Portland girl, long before Gangaji, there was Bolinas. Before the spiritual search led us to India, before we were teachers with foundations to support us, there were just Toni and Eli, two seekers who found each other in an outlaw town on the edge of the continent in the summer of '76.

Toni and I had been together thirteen years before meeting our final teacher. Since falling in love in that first year, we had gone everywhere together and shared every aspect of our life. We started living together when each of us rented a bedroom in a communal household overlooking the Pacific Ocean. I was writing a novel, and we taught Taoist Yoga together in the morning before riding our bikes back into the hills. I would read her my writing and she would heal my traumas from years on the road, searching, with no money or home. I remember once telling her early on, in a riff on Woody Guthrie, that I felt knocked down, kicked in, rolled over, and I hurt all over. Our first year was pure bliss.

The next year we settled in as hippie farmers with chickens, dogs, goats, cats, and a marijuana crop. (See my book *An Outlaw Makes It Home: The Awakening of a Spiritual Revolutionary*.) When neighbor kids started stealing the marijuana, we went to the pound and found a German Shepard that was completely trained, highly intelligent, and funny! Once when we showed him our new baby kittens, he put one in his mouth and looked up at us with an intelligent twinkle.

In the eighties, we moved from the farm to the city, setting up a clinic in San Francisco. I had a private practice in Ericksonian Hypnosis and NLP, and Toni was an acupuncturist, having completed her training in England and then being appointed to the California Board of Examiners for Chinese Medicine.

The Teacher and the Teaching

Since my awakening with LSD, I had been on a search for a teacher who could show me how to pass on what I had realized. This was my mission in life for eighteen years as I passed through different teachings and teachers, fakirs, fakers, gurus, Tibetan Rinpoches, Sufis, and many others. It was during that time that I first saw Toni at Swami Muktananda's ashram in Oakland. I knew she was spiritual as well as knock out gorgeous, and I pursued her.

In 1978, Kalu Rinpoche, the meditation master of the Kagyu lineage of Tibetan Buddhism had a dream about me and appointed me the head of the first Tibetan Dharma center in Marin County, California. Toni was given the name White Tara and appointed an officer of the center.

We spent three years with our Taoist teacher, and among other things, I learned to paint the Tao Teh Ching in Chinese calligraphy, and Toni prepared to be an acupuncturist.

In Marrakesh, Morocco, I was initiated into a Sufi clan of former palace slaves, now trance-dancing together on the full moon.

In the early 1980's, I was presented with a Zen Teaching Fan, permission to transmit the dharma, from O'Jiisan, at the time the oldest living Zen Master, in ChoShoJi Zen Temple, on the island of Kyushu, Japan.

By the time of our clinic, I was leading groups at Esalen, and had published my first book on the Enneagram. We had settled into our life after the farm. We were happy, in love, but still not finished. Our path had not yet come to an end.

We felt a spiritual calling by the end of the decade, closed our offices, sold our Mill Valley home, and moved to a farm in upcountry Maui. We had plans to buy some land and set up a center. We were living on the Maui farm when I set off to find our final teacher in 1990.

* * *

When I knocked on my teacher's door, no one knew me or knew that I was coming. I found him through a series of signs, the final one being local boys flying two kites from the roof above his house. The sweet gentle man who opened the door said, "Come in. He is waiting for you."

I entered a tiny room with a single bed and a small wooden chair. He invited me to sit with him on his bed. In a moment it was over. My mind stopped, my heart opened, and I knew I had met my final teacher. I knew that I was looking at my own self looking back at me with a fire of love burning brightly in his eyes. My eighteen-year spiritual search was over.

I spent the next week alone with a living Buddha. I didn't know how to address him, so at first I called him Babaji, and wrote letters back to Toni about Babaji's transmission of silence and freedom. We ate all our meals together, and at lunch one day he was full and poured the remains of his bowl of baby potatoes into mine. I cried while he laughed, as he said to his son Surendra, the 60-year-old man who had answered the door, "Why does this boy feel like family? Huh?" I was crying and laughing as we passed the mango chutney. I eventually noticed that as his granddaughters cooked for us they called him "Papaji," and so I did as well.

After what seemed an eternity of blissful long walks, meals, and talks, Westerners began arriving for his satsangs. He had me meet

them and guide them to his home in the Narhi Market neighborhood of Lucknow and serve them tea. After the satsangs, he and I would sit together and I would read him my writing of that day's meeting. This was the start of *Wake Up and Roar*.

One day, after three weeks at his side, he took me into his room and said that I had been tested and that I was ready. A week before, I had written to Toni that I was being prepared for a seat in this lineage, and now it was here. I realized in that moment, as I sat at his feet in his tiny bedroom, that I had subconsciously wanted to be a guru just like him.

As I sat there looking up into his eyes, I felt the first movement of pride arising. I stopped him.

"My wife is the satguru," I told him. "Really?" he said. "So rare to find two together. So then, you don't change anything. Just have both therapist and client wake up."

I told him my wife was a goddess not a yogi, so we took the Lucknow Mail, second class sleeper, to the holy river Ganga, to find Toni a suitable room for when I would return with her.

When I returned to India with Toni, he named her Ma Gangaji and said, "She has the purity, nobility, and sattvic nature to take this transmission to the West."

I became her first devotee, the first to call her Gangaji. For the first thirteen years of our relationship, I was the leader; and now that had flipped, and I sat at her feet. She was immaculate as she traveled the world transmitting our teacher's essence of silence and realization.

Perhaps it was inevitable that the ground would shift beneath us. Different forces began pulling at the fabric of our relationship. What had been whole began showing invisible tears.

After years of freedom
I fell into a trap—
A sweeter snare
I never did see.

Beyond lust,
Sentimental delusion.
Heaven to hell
For all to see.

The Unraveling

The Gangaji Foundation had grown up in Boulder to support her teaching, and I stayed on the farm on Maui writing the book I had started in India, *Wake Up and Roar: Satsang with Papaji.*

As Gangaji was leaving the farm for Boulder, we sat on a bench under our avocado tree and spoke of the strong forces pulling us apart.

The people starting the Gangaji Foundation didn't want me around. They wanted their goddess Gangaji to be their guru, without messy partners peeking out from behind the scenes. Although jealous, I could relate. Being replaced at her side by another man, her devoted attendant traveling with her, instead of me, was a burn, but I could bear it.

Our love was being tested and we knew we could weather any storm. I was left on the farm to live with three wild, single hippie women. One had had her baby on the beach in Goa, India, and two were working as massage therapists at the luxury tourist resort's spa down on the beach in Wailea.

Once a small community had come together on our farm, I moved into a one-room cabin down in a pasture because my bedroom, and then the whole farmhouse, became the center of operations for producing tapes of Gangaji's satsangs, supporting my teaching schedule, and publishing my books.

A few months after my beloved was gone, I came into my cabin late one afternoon and there was someone in my bed. She held up the covers to show her naked body and said, "Come on in. It's fine." My first test. I didn't get in bed and asked her to please leave as I backed out the door.

Seven years later, the Portland girl was in my bed.

* * *

By the early nineties, with Gangaji in Boulder, and me on the farm, we had experienced a few years living apart, only coming together for a week or two between Gangaji's travel schedule. It seemed like a lifetime.

One day in 1994, when we both had retreats scheduled in Stinson Beach, California, she saw me hugging one of the women from the farm who was traveling with me as an assistant. Gangaji knew it was time for us to re-bond. She then returned from Boulder and I left the farm as we moved back to where we had started in West Marin. We knew that a gulf had opened between us, and for a time we could not bridge it. I didn't have the insight necessary to address an imbalance that I could not describe. Gangaji was open and willing, but we were stuck in a certain way of relating.

* * *

After the affair, only in retrospect, we realized that there are three levels of our relationship. On the surface, our personalities meshed perfectly. We loved the same museums, movies, books, and food. We loved dancing and making each other laugh. We had loved our sex life, and after fifteen years, neither of us mourned its passing. We had so much in common in our tastes and preferences that life was filled with laughter and bliss. I had first fallen in love when we hiked out of Bolinas to Bass Lake where we swam naked and stoned and made love in the sunshine on the warm grass.

In the depth of our souls we were also perfect partners. We both loved truth most of all. I started as the spiritual teacher, but that role switched in the mid-eighties as her clarity and wisdom deepened and informed my growing self-awareness. At one point, I had fallen at her feet and told her that she was a Satguru, the Sanskrit word for the enlightened teacher who transmits direct realization.

But it was between these two levels that we had problems. It was the level of the subconscious. This was where we told ourselves comments and stories about the other that we would never speak aloud. Somehow there was an imbalance in our relationship that needed to be addressed, and I didn't have the insight to speak it out loud. This was where the affair was born and lived, just below the surface of consciousness.

The body remembers what the mind would forget.
The heart carries what words cannot hold.
Time moves like smoke on the wind,
Bearing seeds of transformation
In its toxic embrace.

Between catastrophe
And consequence—
Silence.
Like breath's pause,
Dawn's threshold,
When truth waits
Unspoken.

The Body Speaks:
Five Years After New York

The consequences of desire rippled out like waves from a stone dropped in still water, touching everyone in its path. The mind may forget, but the body remembers. Mine was about to remind me with a vengeance

In the fall of 2006, my life changed dramatically. For a year, I alternated between attempts at normal activity and not being able to get out of bed. The pain was constant—I told Gangaji it felt like being repeatedly kicked in the ribs while a concrete block crashed onto my skull.

I was also coming out of the most emotionally painful episode of my life.

I had ended my three-year affair in 2005. After exposing the lie in our relationship that I had hid for three years, Gangaji left me—our fifteen-year marriage and thirty years of living together finished. She took off to Australia to teach and get over me. The pain of letting her go was much more severe than anything I would later experience in the cancer ward.

We have two Kate Wolf songs that we have danced to together over the decades, *Brother Warrior* and *Two-Way Waltz*. Alone in the house, having ended both my affair and my marriage, I sobbed uncontrollably. I cried over the pain I had caused and the damage done.

I put on our two songs and danced. I had to cut the limbic bonding that was still holding her back and set her free. As I danced, I was aware on the levels of emotional binding entwining us. We were woven together, our lives knit into a seamless whole. My dancing, the movement of the dance, and the inner light cut away our attachment. It was the most selfless moment of my life and the most painful. I had ruined perfect love. I had destroyed my life and possibility. I discovered that I had been a devotee who had a thought about "me," and ruined everything.

After setting her free, I mourned in despair. I had cut our lifeline and could not pull her back. I lost my true love. I tried to maintain some semblance of normal life. I eventually found a rental, a great old house on the hill overlooking Lithia Park, in Ashland, but I couldn't go through with it. I cancelled my deposit and broke the lease I had just signed. I found I couldn't go on as usual.

I truly had nothing to live for. At first, my life had been devoted to passing on what I had realized. After meeting Papaji and passing on his transmission to Toni, my life mission was accomplished. After that, my life had been devoted to supporting Gangaji, and now I had betrayed that responsibility and devotion with nothing left but despair. For three years, I had lived with the delusion that we three could be a family, that since they both loved me, and I them, we could all three love each other in harmony. Amazing what a supposedly awakened person can believe.

Healing

At some point, maybe a month later, I connected with Gangaji in a dream. I knew I had to see her and I flew to Australia. Gangaji thought I was coming for final goodbyes, but I was going in order to propose. While half asleep on the flight, somewhere over the Pacific Ocean, I left my body and we reconnected. I knew then that our love endured and we could re-bond. In Australia, we met every day for a month to deconstruct and open the secret subconscious stories and bring everything to the light.

That is when we discovered the three levels of relationship and were able to love each other all the way down the line. On December 7th, 2006, we married a second time, but this time with each of us getting a ring. I wore mine for a decade longer than she, but gave it up once it was clear that we were moving from Senior to Elder to now Old, and she could again trust me not to move.

Returning from Australia, Gangaji and I met with my ex-lover and, after some time, we three reconciled. Gangaji and I were begged to keep the affair a secret because of her fear of judgement by the community. Although we wanted full disclosure, we honored her request, and through it all Gangaji was impeccable. Her clarity, wisdom, and compassion never wavered in her support of truth and forgiveness.

A year later the revelation of the affair went viral. I experienced the hatred and projections of negativity from people I had never met, as well as some in my community. By keeping a secret, I had implicitly lied to keep the affair hidden. Since I had never spoken about it, or verbally denied it, I hadn't seen that I was lying. I believed my private life was no one else's business, part of my subconscious justification that ran the story. More than the affair, this secrecy was what shattered our community.

The previous year, I had felt the pain I had caused to my partner and my lover. The personal pain of the suffering I had caused, particularly to those I claimed to love, decades after taking Bodhisattva vows to end suffering, shattered all inflated ideas of myself. I was crushed and humbled in surrender. Then, a year later, there was the public flaying.

When by chance we met, I asked my ex-lover what had happened to trigger this reversal. She told me that she went to a therapist because she still loved me and was suffering. The therapist "educated" her by telling her she had been in a cult and was suffering from Stockholm Syndrome, where the captive falls in love with the jailer. With her therapist's guidance, she realized that she had been hypnotized and abused. She was sent to cult deprogramming and now seemed to have a new reality, with new memories, and a mission to start a crusade to save other women from her fate.

I had promised my now ex-lover, as we were separating and she was begging me to stay, that I would carry the pain in my bones forever. And so, I did. I assumed that the crushing pain of feeling I was being kicked and of having a concrete weight dropped on my head were the karma of my situation. It felt like the psychic attacks of a witch hunt had manifested in an attack on my body, and I took the blows. It went on for almost a year, continuing to worsen in severity.

My teaching fell away as pain consumed me. Because of my deep commitment to alternative healing and avoiding Western medicine, I spent eight months with acupuncture, body work, and herbs to address the bone-deep pain, but nothing worked.

By June 2007, at sixty years old, as I was preparing for my trip to Europe to meet Gangaji and start our annual retreat, the pain got much worse. My chiropractor and my doctor teamed up and had an intervention with me. They both "respected my autonomy" and my "freedom of choice," but at this stage I really needed to get an MRI before flying out of the country.

The test results were stark: besides a fractured rib and lesions from the top of my head to my hips, stress fractures in my spine had caused me to lose three inches in height. The surgeon described my spine as showing the severe osteoporosis of an eighty-year-old woman. This led to both vertebral surgery and a biopsy, revealing last-stage multiple myeloma—an aggressive blood cancer I'd never heard of, though it would soon seem to appear everywhere I looked.

My research revealed grim statistics: two-thirds of patients died within three years; half of the remaining third within two years after that. Yet understanding finally brought peace—my suffering now had a name, a context beyond my personal betrayal and the attacks that followed.

Body's crucible—
Truth born of pain,
Wisdom from weakness,
Strength through surrender.
All falls away.

What remains:
Truth's marrow,
Bone-knowing
Love and loss
As one flame.

The Journey to Little Rock

I n this unlikely place, I would meet the first of two unlikely healers who would save my life.

As I researched where to go for treatment, I noticed that most published research papers, by far, were coming out of Arkansas. This was a shock. I had expected to go for treatment to either the west or east coast. In an unexpected twist, my path led to Little Rock, Arkansas—amazingly, at the time, the nation's epicenter for multiple myeloma research. An oncologist, a member of our satsang community had heard of my cancer and knew the head of the Myeloma Institute in Little Rock. He contacted me and introduced me to my future doctor.

Though I'd never stepped foot in a Walmart and opposed its corporate values, I owe my life to Sam Walton. Before his death from multiple myeloma, he had established the world's leading research and treatment center at the University of Arkansas Medical School in Little Rock, a little way down the road from his Bentonville home.

Sam Walton brought my doctor-to-be, Bart Barlogie, from Heidelberg, Germany, to run the program. He was a renegade genius who rode his motorcycle to work, wore his leathers in his office, and asked to be called Bart. He gave me his email and his cell phone number. I could text him anytime for the next decade and he would reply within minutes. He has since retired, but we are still in contact. Bart saved my life and I love him and deeply treasure him.

One of the breakthroughs of the Arkansas team, in studying the genetics of the disease, is that they were able to successfully determine if the cause was genetic or environmental. They found that genetic causes were more difficult to treat with a shorter survival time. The doctors told me the "good news" that the cause of my cancer was environmental.

While they didn't follow up with the term "the bad news," they went on to describe my condition metaphorically: a ten-alarm fire raged in my bones. Life expectancy was statistically three years from diagnosis but, perhaps because of my years of trying alternative medicine, I had already made it to the last stage of the disease without Western medical intervention. I had used up a lot of my remaining time.

I enrolled in Bart's experimental protocol and relocated to Little Rock for six months of intensive treatment. As I underwent treatment, reports emerged of firemen and first responders from Ground Zero dying of multiple myeloma. The same toxic brew that had altered my genes was claiming others, but without proof of causation, insurance companies denied their claims. It broke my heart that I was covered by insurance and in the best hands, while they, who deserved all coverage and care, were dying without treatment for a lack of causal proof.

Bart was always surrounded by an international team of oncologists accompanying him on his rounds in order to learn his unique protocol. Sometimes it could seem that he was suffering from Tourette's as he would blurt out biting, very edgy humorous remarks to break the somber mood. He once insulted a Syrian doctor by teasing him, calling him a "camel jockey," to which the Syrian doc replied, "Yes, my people were riding camels while your

Dr. Bart Barlogie and me in Little Rock.

people were still eating the bark off the trees." We had some good laughs in the chemo labs.

Bart's experimental protocol defied conventional wisdom. Where standard treatment used minimal chemotherapy, his approach pushed the body to its limits, using maximum dosages coupled with two stem-cell transplants. Each new round of chemo began before I'd recovered from the last, creating a relentless assault on the cancer.

The protocol was brutal, but the biopsies were worse. They were the most painful part of the process, without a second. It was still Arkansas, and the staff assigned to biopsies may have wandered in from a cafeteria job looking for work and got stuck in the basement doing a job that no one wanted. It may have been on the job training. If so, I hope that what they learned in trial and error and practice on me was useful for someone else. The pain of having a very large and long needle drilled into my lower back to penetrate the lumbar spine and extract the marrow was extreme. Having incompetent people missing the mark, having to start over, causing secondary pain, and prolonging the procedure, was excruciating.

At one point, with my marrow 80% compromised, my bones were so soft that they were breaking off on contact with the needle, keeping the technicians from getting a clean draw as they tried again and again, generating relentless waves of sharp pain. It seemed like endless hours as they tried and failed. But, as bad as it was, I would rather repeat that than the emotional pain of the betrayal of Gangaji.

One of Bart's major breakthroughs came from a conference he had attended where two Israeli doctors reported on a unique effect in their work with leprosy patients. Looking for a cheap sedative, they came across thalidomide. Thalidomide was developed in Switzerland and Germany in the 1950s as a sedative for pregnant mothers. Unfortunately, it caused an epidemic of severely deformed babies and was quickly abandoned. Apparently, these doctors had warehouses of it at their disposal and a non-breeding population. They reported that the thalidomide not only eased anxiety but, in some cases, stopped or even reversed the symptoms of leprosy. The theory being that the drug killed off fast growing cells, like embryos and the wasting of leprosy.

Bart successfully developed his experimental mix, including thalidomide, in his multi-drug protocol to kill off the fast-replicating cancer cells. While it saved lives, the toxic brew also caused secondary disease and made my body forcibly reject food. When

I first began treatment, they gave me three different anti-nausea medications, a shot, and two pills, but nothing worked. The first few days, I threw up everywhere on everything.

Though still illegal in most states, I had access to one of the country's first medical marijuana programs. The Goddess of Marijuana came to the rescue. When in my condo, with towels under the door, I could use a vaporizer with my homegrown, but at the hospital I used a little vial of drops. It was so effective, I never threw up again. I shared my report with the docs and nurses. One of the Lebanese oncologists was brave enough to take one of my offered golden buds and later reported how much he liked the clarity of the high. No one else would touch it, but the nurses guided me to a patient who was wasting away and not able to tolerate the chemo. I rolled her joints and had to have a long talk to convince her that she would not become addicted and it wasn't against God. I was later told that she survived.

Between diagnosis and destiny
Lies a landscape of choices
That look nothing like choosing.
Each step forward a surrender,
Each surrender a step.
The path appears
Beneath feet willing
To walk into darkness,
Trusting the ground
They cannot see.

The Battle

At some point, while I struggled to get out of bed, trembling and trying to rise on an elbow, my sweetheart caretaker Patrick, who had shown up to relieve Gangaji so she could continue her teaching schedule, looked at me and said, "Stay down Rocky! Stay down." And we laughed together in the face of death.

During my darkest moment, too weak to retrieve a fallen pillow, I did face my death. My only regret, which I mourned, was my lack of life insurance—a consequence of my risk-taking, anti-authoritarian nature—and felt I'd failed as a provider to my beloved partner. Yet our love had weathered every storm, growing purer with each trial. I found myself complete, ready for whatever path love chose.

While I was hairless and bloated, unable to walk up a flight of stairs, in a wheelchair with congestive heart disease brought on by the chemo, a neighbor and fellow patient in the condo complex went out for a round of golf. The next day he was dead.

When the port was inserted, I had asked the person doing the procedure how long the port would be in my body. He said the pump had a five-year expiration date but that he had never taken any out. "So, five years or death of the body. Whichever comes first."

While lying in bed too weak to move and facing the end, I reached for a yellow legal pad in the hope that something worthwhile would come from my death that would benefit others. If these

Gangaji and me with my new port.

were to be my final teachings, let them come from the marrow of truth itself. These songs of freedom flowed out, echoing ancient rhythms, but speaking my own experience.

Body's crucible—
Truth born of pain,
Wisdom from weakness,
Strength through surrender.
All falls away.

What remains:
Truth's marrow,
Bone deep-knowing
Love and loss
As one flame.

Songs of Freedom

Lines on Water

Nothing is real.
Everything else comes and goes.
Nothing is certain.
Everything else a gamble.
Nothing is perfect.
Everything else
Makes mistakes.

We are a symphony of Love
Learning by sounding wrong notes.

Don't fall into the mistaken belief
That we are not separate
Don't fall into the mistaken belief
That we are not One.
Both and neither
Are included in reality.

Meet emptiness with silence—
All is revealed.

The Fire of Love

I wanted to change the world.
Instead, the world changed me.
It tore me open,
Like a walnut
From a green shell.

Love left me beaten and battered,
With my bones ground to dust.
How grateful I am
For this holy fire

That bares the tender sweetness
In the midst of destruction.

I bow in gratitude.

The Trap of Ego

To give up being right—
The ego's great challenge.
Be willing
And not knowing.
All is revealed.

Defeats are the teacher.
Sweet victories the snare.
Be willing to bear both
Without moving,
And the bliss
Will seem overwhelming.

Another trap
On the path
Of the free.

Bear both
Without moving.
Bliss will flood emptiness,
Celebrating in prostration.

Selfishness is a hungry ghost
Always searching for more
Bringing bad fortune on oneself and others
While afraid of Freedom's door.
Your Self is not selfish

Be yourself and see.
Natural selflessness
Is the sweetest bliss
Comforting all
With the balm of the free.

Mind

The open mind does not push
And does not resist
And does not
Just go with the flow.

The open mind reveals what is immovable.
Implacable.
A fair witness.
A servant of Love
Making tea.

Surrender and Freedom

You are already chosen.
You have nowhere to go.
Simply stop here
Without moving.
All will be revealed.

Your nature is pure.
Your heart is holy.
Your being is Love.
Your song a song of freedom.
Sing it uniquely
From the depths of your soul.

Merge into the Beloved.
Appear unchanged
And unchanging.
Let the mystery have you,
And your life
Will be unimaginable.

Open your grasp,
And all is yours.
Close your grasp,
And it all slips away.

Be yourself
And be free.

Love is the Master

Love is the master.
Love is the student.
Love is the teaching.
Love is the realization.

Love is a ruthless killer.
Love takes no prisoners.
Love demands full surrender.

Without compromise
Or deal making.

True surrender
Is a surrender to Love
Already alive and free
As your heart.

Surrender needs nothing
And uses everything
For its purpose.

Be free and see.

Love appearing as grace
Can't resist kissing you.
This kiss is a fatal embrace.
All that came before disappears.

The mind is terrified
Of this death.
The soul dances
In full prostration at the good news.
Which do you serve?

Serving Love
Is love's greatest joy.
Serving Love
Leads to insight, revelation
And abiding peace.

All else
Is chasing shadows in the graveyard.
Be yourself and see.

Virtue

Virtue is a noble aspect of love.
It is surrendered and silent
Completely uncompromising
Gentle and forgiving.

Virtue stands
In the midst of confusion
As a resting place
Silently announcing
All minds are welcome
To come and be still.

To celebrate virtue is a service of love.
Celebration requires no practice.
There are no do-overs in this spiral of life.
We go around without going back
And without ever leaving.

Be what you would practice
Be yourself and see.

The Shadow Play

All of life
Is a shadow play.
When the full sun of love
Is revealed,
The shadows disappear.

Ages of beliefs fall away
In the light of freedom.
Shadows of superstition
And faith disappear
At the speed of sight.

Touched
With luminosity,
There is no need
For candles in the dark
Or shepherds herding sheep.

The light of love
Knows itself
Without question or doubt.
It needs no foundation
Or external illumination.
It stands alone.

The Symphony of Love

We are all
A symphony of Love,
Learning
By sounding
Wrong notes.

We are
The music of the spheres,
Literally alive
As soundless space.

We are
The almost unbearable
Roar of Silence.

Be yourself and see.

The Pain of Illusion

When all the world
Turns against you,
Maybe they are right.
Be willing to see,
And all is revealed.

Love is trustworthy
Beyond doubt or belief.
Love
Has love's
Best interests at heart.

Be love,
And others
Will naturally
Find their way.
All ideals

Are illusion.
The pain
Of dying to our illusions
Is the great disillusion.
We avoid
Being disillusioned
At all costs.

We pay with our lives.

I was a childish idealist
For much of my life.
I loved "the people"
And hated individuals.
I loved the ideal
And hated selfishness
And greed.
This was a veil
Imposed
On holy perfection.

All hatred
Is self-hatred.
Better to surrender
And see.

Death as an Ally

After freedom's years
I fell into a trap—
A sweeter snare
I never did see.

Beyond lust,
Sentimental delusion.
Heaven to hell
For all to see.

Dark night of the soul
Brings Death as an ally.
Not for escape
But to set one free.

Meeting Death
Face on
Reveals
Deeper silence.
Once reborn
There are other
Deaths to meet.

We want to avoid it,
This blessing of dying
And the pain of birth
That reveals fresh clarity.

Fate is in charge.
Our preferences meaningless.
Love carries us Home
Upright and free.

Freedom

Freedom
Is the holy goal
That leads to deeper realization.
To be free is the rarest gem
That love bestows.

The animal is never free.
The animal is bound by time and space.
The animal is bound by its need to feed.
It is not the animal that becomes free.

What is free is already ever free.
It is causeless and useless.
It is the supreme gift of a lifetime
That can never be achieved.

What can be shed
Is the identity of the animal.
Be free and see.

Freedom has no precedent or requirement
Therefore it is free.
Freedom is not bound by society
Nor in defiance of society's appearance
Therefore it is free.
Freedom is not dependent
On circumstance or special favor
Therefore it is free.

Life's adventure is not for the wary
Stop imagining a future
Allow your heart to lead.
Calling you home
It is the ferry for the free.

Let Truth have you fully
And you will realize directly
What is always free.

A Living Example

Don't shout down liars and thieves
Rather be the living example
This is a service of Love.

A living example does not preach
Does not need to show others
The error of their ways.

A living example
Does not proclaim righteousness
A clanging in the ears of Love.

A living example
Is flexible, has no dogma.
A living example
Is grateful to serve
Not through practice
Nor ideas of what is right
But simply by being naturally yourself.

A living example
Does what she loves.

The Choice to Be Free

Is free will possible
In the midst of conditioning?
Not until the choice
Is made to be free.
All else endless wandering
In the dream of free will
As all are washed out to sea.

The choice to be free
Is setting the fire
That burns up the past,
The future and "me."

What cannot be burned
Is ever burning
Shining in pure bliss
And deep harmony.

From karma to dharma
The momentum continues
Setting the stage for the tests
And the beauty.

Each life
An art form
In the eyes
Of the Beloved.

Each life
A momentary sparkle
On the cosmic sea.

Each life meaningless
And filled with meaning
If the dreamer is sought
Behind the scenes.

The fire that forges
Is the fire that frees.
The wound that breaks us
Is the crack where light shines.

All paths
Lead here—

This moment,
This silence,
This awakening
To grace's
Relentless love.

Full Circle:
The Fire Still Burns

Today, standing in my garden in the crisp morning air, I think back to that toxic wind that swept through my apartment near Ground Zero. The acrid smell of destruction has long since dissipated, but the memory remains sharp—a reminder of how quickly life can flip. Back then, I witnessed how catastrophe could either shut hearts down or blow them wide open. I didn't know that my own catastrophe, seeded by a breeze, waited in the wings, ready to teach me the same lesson in an intimately personal way. I carry the scars of many fires—some chosen, some thrust upon me. Each has left its mark; each has offered its teaching.

After six months in Arkansas, when it looked like the treatment was working, I was discharged with a port in my chest for weekly, and then monthly, chemo. The port stayed with me for six years—a year beyond its expiration date. When the time finally came to remove it, I sat in the same procedure room where I'd once asked about its lifespan. The technician who had matter-of-factly told me "five years or death of the body, whichever comes first" wasn't there to witness this victory. Instead, a new technician gently removed the device that had been both my lifeline and a constant reminder of mortality. The small scar it left behind became another testament to survival, joining the constellation of marks across my body that tell the story of my journey.

Just as my experience in Little Rock showed me that healing could come from unexpected places, my journey with cancer revealed that transformation often arrives in packages we'd never choose for ourselves. Western medicine, which I had once regarded with such skepticism, had saved my life.

The final twist in my healing journey came in 2017. Donny Yance, a master herbalist specializing in cancer treatment, discovered the key to my healing. Bart's protocols, prolonged my life long enough for a new generation of discovery and drugs to appear. Where Western medicine had kept me alive, ancient herbal wisdom, coupled with the latest biotechnology, would help complete the cure.

Gene deletions, I learned, are fragments of genes blown out or turned off by trauma. By analyzing my gene deletions, which were blown out from 9/11, and the root cause of my myeloma, Donny found a new-generation experimental drug that could attack the protein structures of my remaining cancer cells. It was not approved for use in myeloma, but the evidence he found pointed to it working. I arranged a phone call between Donny and Bart, and Bart was amazed. Bart wanted Donny to come and join him at Mount Sinai in New York, where he had been hired as the research director. I hadn't told Bart that Donny was an herbalist. If he had known, Bart would never have taken the call.

Donny brought western medicine and herbal tradition back full circle into full harmony. Bart got me the meds and within weeks my numbers of active cancer cells dropped to normal and have not returned. I am now number fifty on Mount Sinai's survivors list.

The "ten-alarm fire" that once raged in my bones has been quenched, but another kind of fire continues to burn. It's the same fire I saw in 1976 when my partner and I first made love. It was in my teacher's eyes in India. It was there in those days after 9/11, when New Yorkers opened their homes and hearts to strangers. It's the fire that sustained me through the darkest days of treatment, when love proved stronger than fear. It's the fire that burns away illusion and leaves only what is real and true.

My body bears the marks of battle—the collapsed vertebrae that left me shorter and stooped with twists in my spine; the bone lesions that remind me of my vulnerability. Yet these are also markers of a profound gift: the opportunity to live fully the teachings that had long filled my mind and heart, but needed to reach my bones. The cancer forced me to fully embody the surrender I had been sinking into for years.

In my earlier life, I had been a teacher of freedom, but cancer became one of my teachers. It showed me that true freedom isn't found in escape from life's harsh realities, but in full acceptance of them. In truth, when I first received the diagnosis that predicted mortality, the ending of my life seemed like a reprieve. I imagined a cautionary tale that *hatred kills* would live on as my legacy.

Death seemed an escape from humiliation. I was relieved at the thought of dying, but my commitment to my partner and my promise not to die first, had a higher priority. The disease I once thought would be my ending became instead a new beginning—a fierce invitation to live more fully, love more deeply, and finally understand that our wounds and our healing are one and the same.

Now, eighteen years past the original three-year prognosis, I stand as living testament to both medical innovation and the mysterious ways of grace. What began as a death sentence became an invitation to deeper life.

These days, my teaching continues, deepened by fire. My teacher said, "Vigilance to the last breath. You are on a razor's edge, so don't carry a load. Even one thought is a load." After twelve years of silent bliss, I had picked up a thought in the first seeding of desire and had to live the consequences of that bitter fruit.

I once made a prayer to myself while sitting with my teacher in his bedroom in India—that all of my flaws be revealed so that I could be a more perfect devotee to his silent transmission. Luckily, I had no idea at the time of the prayer that they all would be exposed on a public stage, or I might have hedged my prayer with a conditional sidebar for privacy.

The insights into myself, my capacity for self-deception, and my willingness to live and to die for truth, are embodied in every scar and victory. Students who find their way to me find a lighter of candles informed by life's raw reality and the facing of my human flaws.

During my twelve years of celibacy, a sense of superiority gradually grew inflated. Only in retrospect could I see the spiritual arrogance that had entered my life. It sometimes had tainted my teaching. All now ground to dust in humility and shame.

The fire of love still burns. It burns in every moment of borrowed time, in every breath that exceeds the statistical predictions, in every sunrise I'm privileged to witness. It burns in the deepened relationship with my partner, tempered and strengthened by all we've weathered together. It burns in my continued amazement at life's mysterious ways—how the same force that can break us open can also reveal our essential wholeness.

I've learned that transformation rarely arrives as we imagine it should. Sometimes it comes as a toxic wind blowing through an open door. Sometimes it comes as a diagnosis we never wanted to hear. Sometimes it comes as love that breaks us open when we thought we were already broken enough. But always, if we can stay present to it, transformation comes as an invitation to discover what in us is truly indestructible.

This then is our mission and challenge in this deeply wounded world: to recognize that our personal stories, however painful or triumphant, are doorways to something deeper. When we surrender our narratives of self, we discover the silent, intelligent truth beyond all stories. In realizing this, we become living lights of love, shining from the depths of emptiness and silence. Through this conscious awakening, we embody the possibility of human realization and peace.

As our world burns in destruction caused by ego, fear, selfishness, arrogance, ignorance, and rage, with most of our people trapped in false religions and cults, one candle lights the darkness around it and the light spreads from heart to heart as candles light candles light candles until the dawn comes after the blackest night.

To those who might find these words in their own dark night: your journey will be uniquely your own, but you are not alone. The fire that seems to be destroying your life may be the very flame that will illuminate your path home. Trust it. Let it do its work. Let it show you, as it showed me, that love is indeed the master, and that freedom isn't found in escaping our humanity, but in embracing it fully, with all its pain and all its glory.

Just as I flew into New York that September day, witnessing both destruction and rebirth, we are all flying into unknown territories of transformation. The fire still burns, and I remain grateful for its light—now not just as witness, but as living proof of love's enduring grace.

The fire of truth continues to spread. Gangaji shares this invitation to peace with people from all walks of life offering her retreats, online programs, and podcasts through the Gangaji Foundation. Her retreats and global online gatherings bring together over 1,000 people each month from more than forty countries, while her podcasts are downloaded in more than 150 countries. In addition, the Gangaji Foundation Prison Program serves and supports the spiritual inquiry of men and women living behind bars. Gangaji's course for inmates, *Freedom Inside*, is accessible in more than 1,400 US prisons. Currently over 5,000 prisoners are drinking in a profound and simple message—no matter where you may find yourself, you have the capacity to discover yourself as peace and freedom itself. To learn more about Gangaji and her programs visit www.gangaji.org.

I continue to train therapists, which I had been doing whenI first met Papaji. He gave me a directive and a mission. On our first walk together, holding hands, he said, "A candle that lights other candles is one thing. But a candle that lights other candles that light other candles is something else." The Leela School of Awakening is dedicated to that mission. www.leelaschool.org

gangaji.org

leelaschool.org

Also by Eli Jaxon-Bear

Fixation to Freedom: The Enneagram of Liberation (2025)

The Awakened Guide: A Manual for Leaders, Teachers, Coaches, Healers and Helpers (2020)

An Outlaw Makes It Home: The Awakening of a Spiritual Revolutionary (2018)

Wake Up and Roar: Satsang with Papaji (1992, 2016)

Sudden Awakening: Stop Your Mind, Open Your Heart, and Discover Your True Nature (2001, 2015)

Lied der Freiheit (1998)

Cosmic Jokes and Teaching Stories (1990)

Healing the Heart of Suffering: Using the Enneagram for Spiritual Growth (1989)

www.ingramcontent.com/pod-product-compliance
Lightning Source LLC
Chambersburg PA
CBHW020421150626
46554CB00014B/2310